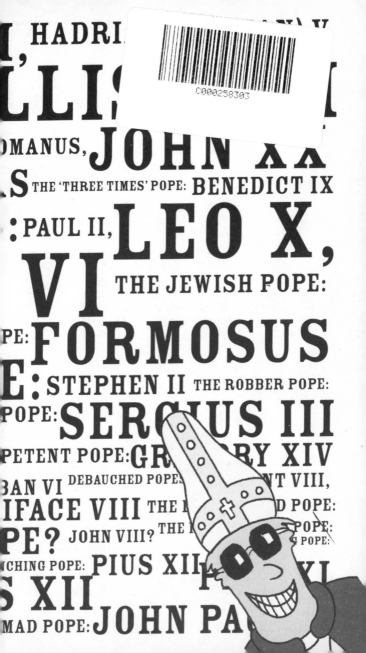

# Holy Smoke

**Bob Curran** is an educational psychologist at the University of Ulster, Coleraine. He also works extensively in community education and with adults in return-to-education schemes. His community-based approach links him with the history and folklore of many areas all over Ireland. His interests are broad-ranging but are focused especially on history and story. He has written several books, including *The Field Guide to Irish Fairies*, *The Wolfhound Guide to the Shamrock*, *Creatures of Celtic Myth*, *The Truth about the Leprechaun*, *A Haunted Land: Ireland's Ghosts* and *A Bewitched Land: Ireland's Witches, Wise Women and Warlocks*.

# HOLY SMOKE!

## TRUE PAPAL STORIES THAT WILL AMAZE AND AMUSE

Bob Curran

ILLUSTRATED BY DONAL O'DEA

THE O'BRIEN PRESS
DUBLIN

First published 2006 by The O'Brien Press Ltd,
20 Victoria Road, Dublin 6, Ireland.
Tel: +353 1 4923333; Fax: +353 1 4922777
E-mail: books@obrien.ie
Website: www.obrien.ie

ISBN-10: 0-86278-947-8
ISBN-13: 978-0-86278-947-3

British Library Cataloguing-in-Publication Data
Curran, Bob
Holy Smoke : the unholy truth from history
1.Popes 2.Papacy - History
I.Title II.O'Dea, Donal
262.1'3'0922

1 2 3 4 5 6 7 8
06 07 08 09 10

*Amare et sapere vix deo conceditur*

Editing, typesetting, layout, design: The O'Brien Press Ltd
Printing: Reálszisztéma Dabas Printing House, Hungary

# STRUCK-OFF POPES

## John XXIII
### 3 MAY 1410–29 MAY 1415

This is *not* the pope who took the name in 1958 but a pontiff who ruled 500 years earlier. John, born Baldassare Cossa, was an 'embarrassment' to the Church, deemed guilty of incest, adultery and homicide. He also kept his brother's wife in the Vatican as his mistress.

He was deposed by decree of the Council of Constance in 1415 – effectively 'impeached' and his name excised from the list of popes. He was sent as a punishment to Tusculum as Cardinal-Bishop, where he is said to have seduced over 200 nuns, impregnating a number of them. When Bishop Angelo Roncalli decided to take the name in 1958, it caused something of a constitutional alarm.

## Hadrian (Adrian) V
### JULY–AUGUST 1276

Hadrian V was removed from the list of popes by a ruling of Pope Paul VI in November 1975, on the grounds that he had never been ordained even as a priest. Born Ottobono Feishchi, he was the 'nephew' (more likely the illegitimate son) of Pope Innocent IV and a deacon in the Church of San Adriano, hence his papal name.

He also served as Legate to England before returning to Rome. Through a mixture of bribery and family connections he became a member of the College of Cardinals, although he was not a cardinal, and later became Pope. He died of a serious illness in Viterbo, north of Rome, just weeks after taking office.

# THE EX-CON POPE

**Callistus I**
**217–222**

Regarded as a violent and aggressive pope, Callistus had once started a fight in a church on the Sabbath, for which he had been arrested, tried and convicted to one year's hard labour in the salt mines in Sardinia. There he was widely regarded as a bullying criminal.

This conviction and his bad reputation did not, of course, prevent him from becoming Pope in 217, nor did it prevent him from being made a saint.

# THE SUED POPE

**Paul VI**
**21 JUNE 1963–6 AUGUST 1978**

California law student William Sheffield successfully sued the Pope over the sum of $428.50. Sixty dollars of this had been paid to a Swiss monastery as a down payment for a St Bernard dog which had not been delivered. He therefore sued the Pope as head of the Roman Catholic Church.

Sheffield was awarded the full price of the dog by an Alemeda County superior judge who counted the Pope as 'the managing director of the firm selling the dog' and therefore liable for its business obligations.

Sheffield is the only person in history ever to have successfully sued the Papacy but, although now a lawyer in Santa Ana, he has never been able to collect his judgment. The newspaper headline writers of the time, however, had a field day, with one proclaiming, 'Vatican Is Dogmatic In Court'.

# NONEXISTENT POPES

### Romanus
**AUGUST–NOVEMBER 897**

Following the upheavals which followed the *Synod Horrenda* (see The Exhumed Pope), Rome was split into a number of factions. The pontiff Stephen VI(I) (May 896–August 897), who was clearly mad, was quickly deposed, imprisoned and strangled to death, provoking threats of civil revolt in the Holy City.

A pontiff named Romanus was hastily elected, though who he was and where he came from are unknown. He issued no edicts and vacated Peter's Seat after only two months. What became of him is also unknown, as is the date of his death. Unusually for an allegedly Italian pope, he is not buried in St Peter's.

It is possible that 'Romanus' was simply a name put about by the Vatican as a 'holding tactic' to prevent revolution until a new pope could be elected and that nobody actually sat on the Papal Throne. Scholars have noted the similarity between the Pope's name and that of the Holy City itself. Romanus was succeeded by Theodore II, who reigned for only twenty days.

## John XX

During the tenth and eleventh centuries the name John was the most popular – and unlucky – papal choice. When John XXIII was elected in 1958, however, it had not been used for over seven centuries.

The frequency of the name created confusion in the medieval Vatican records, so that when Petrus Hispanus (Peter of Spain – the only Portuguese Pope and the only doctor ever to have been made Pontiff) was elected in September 1276, officials insisted that he take the name John XXI, even though there hadn't been a John XX. This was, it is thought, to rectify some discrepancy in earlier records. Although the name 'John XX' appears in some religious rolls, no dates are given for him, as he never existed.

# MARRIED POPES

### Hormisdas
**20 JULY 514–6 AUGUST 523**

Although today we tend to think of popes as celibate, this has not always been the case. It is thought that a number of the early pontiffs were married; a good number certainly had mistresses. Some popes were even the fathers and grandfathers of others. Pope Hormisdas, for example, was the father of Pope Silverius (536–537), whilst Gregory I (Gregory the Great, 590–604) is thought to have been the great-grandson of Felix III (483–492).

Hadrian (Adrian) II (867–872), who was lame and blind in one eye, was certainly married before becoming Pope and had a daughter. In spite of severe criticism he kept both wife and child in the Lateran Palace. Shortly after moving in, they were kidnapped and the Pope appealed to the French king Louis II for help in tracing them, whereupon the kidnappers murdered both.

Although not formally married themselves, many pontiffs were not above consorting with married women. John XII, for example, is believed to have suffered a fatal heart attack in May 964 whilst in bed with another man's wife. It is possible, however, that he may have been beaten to death by the woman's irate husband. His demise was formally ascribed to 'exhaustion in the pursuance of his office'.

# THE 'THREE TIMES' POPE

## Benedict IX
**21 OCTOBER 1032–SEPTEMBER 1044;**
**10 MARCH–1 MAY 1045;**
**8 NOVEMBER 1047–16 JULY 1048**

Only one man has held the Papacy on three separate occasions. Benedict IX (born Theophylact) followed his father John XIX to St Peter's Chair when he was only fourteen. His election was manifestly arranged through bribery.

Once Pope, he led a wholly immoral life, indulging himself with mistresses and handing out favours and Church positions to members of his own family. At last, in September 1044, the Roman people threatened to revolt against Papal rule and Benedict fled the city. Whilst he was gone, a rival family installed one of its members as Pope Sylvester III.

However, Benedict had never been formally deposed. Despite having recently married, he managed to excommunicate Sylvester as a heretic and reclaim Peter's Chair. He promptly divorced his wife and took a mistress, but within two months he was bored with the Papacy and considered remarrying the wife whom he'd abandoned. He therefore sold the Papacy to his grandfather, John Gratian, who took the name Gregory VI.

The new Pope now faced Sylvester III again, and each pope declared the other a heretic. Benedict, realising his mistake, wanted to buy the Papacy back. In the autumn of 1046, Emperor Henry III, wishing to be crowned by a *legitimate* pope, convened a synod at Sutri near Rome, and summoned the three contenders to it. On Christmas Eve 1046, Henry and his synod deposed them all and declared Suidger of Bamburg as Pope. He took the name Clement II, but his reign lasted only eight months when he suddenly and inexplicably died (some say that he was poisoned).

The Roman people, no doubt encouraged by bribes, now demanded that Benedict be returned as Pope. He was reinstated on 8 November 1047, but only remained in office until 16 July 1048, when he was deposed once more by Emperor Henry III. All these unedifying events took place before Benedict was even thirty.

Henry installed the German Peppo of Brixen as Pope Damasus II and Benedict retreated to his Tusculan homeland where he continued to regard himself as Pope, issuing edicts and denouncing Damasus and his successor Leo IX as heretics.

Summoned to appear before a Lateran Council on a charge of simony (the buying and selling of spiritual goods and church offices), he refused and was excommunicated. He promptly excommunicated every member of the Council who had summoned him but his edicts were now invalid. He would live another seven and a half years and would be buried, not in St Peter's, but in the abbey church of Gottaferrata in the Alban hills.

# PLAYBOY POPES

## Paul II
### 30 AUGUST 1464–26 JULY 1471

Although there could be a number of serious contenders for the title 'top playboy pope', Paul II must count as one of the front-runners. Born Pietro Barbo in 1417, he was the nephew of Pope Eugenius IV, ensuring him a rapid rise in the Church hierarchy. He was arguably the worst of the Renaissance pontiffs – vain, intellectually shallow and extremely ostentatious in his lifestyle.

He was a promoter of carnivals, to which expense he forced Roman Jews to contribute under pain of attack and closure of their businesses. He ran what today would be described as extortion and racketeering enterprises all across Rome and consorted with the city's criminals.

Like some of his predecessors, Paul tried to mount a crusade against the expanding Turkish Empire and called on Christian kings to support him financially. His efforts bore little fruit, however, as he himself pocketed most of the money.

The King of Bohemia eventually suspected what he was doing and threatened to expose him, whereupon Paul excommunicated the King on the grounds that he was a Hussite (Protestant). Others who opposed Paul or spoke out against his playboy ways were arrested and tortured, as

Paul brooked no opposition. He died suddenly from a stroke at the age of fifty-four.

The Vatican Librarian, whom the Pope had bullied and tortured, took his revenge during the next pontificate by publishing a highly unflattering biography of Paul II.

## Leo X
### 17 MARCH 1513–1 DECEMBER 1521

Giovanni de Medici (the son of Lorenzo the Magnificent) must also figure as a 'playboy pope', if only because of the amount of money that he squandered on himself and his surroundings. He had the floors of several of his palaces inlaid with gold. His banquets were the talk of Rome and he kept a private circus.

Leo had been made a priest at the age of seven and a cardinal at the age of thirteen. He was a Renaissance prince who loved fine wines, books, art, music, theatre and spectacle. He was determined to make Rome the cultural centre of Europe. Soon the Papacy was in serious debt and Leo was forced to sell off many Vatican treasures in order to meet his mounting bills.

Worse was to come. The Turkish Empire was expanding and Leo was forced, by a number of Christian kings, to call a crusade to limit its power. To finance this and also the building of a new St Peter's, he had to borrow on a mammoth scale and to institute what would now be called a 'bargain sale' of Church offices, including cardinals' hats.

Even this did not bring in enough money and he began selling 'indulgences' – forgiveness for sins before they had been committed – in the wealthy German diocese of Brandenburg and Mainz. Leo appointed John Tetzel to preach the indulgences in January 1517 and, in response, a German monk, Martin Luther, posted his Ninety-five theses on the church door at Wittenberg, laying the foundations for the Protestant Reformation.

Seemingly unperturbed, Leo continued his extravagant lifestyle, further infuriating the reformers. He largely ignored the building spiritual crisis in the Church, in favour of hunting, lavish banquets and the development of the city as a cultural and hedonistic centre. As a religious storm broke around him Leo suddenly died in 1521 from malaria, leaving Italy in political turmoil and all the problems of the Church to his successor, the Dutchman Hadrian (Adrian) VI.

## Clement VI
### 7 MAY 1342–6 DECEMBER 1352

Very few of the vicars of Christ can outdo the French Pope Clement VI for hedonism, drinking or living the good life. It was during Clement's reign that the expression 'drunk as a pope' was coined and it certainly reflected the easy-going, worldly style of this playboy pope.

Clement reigned at a time when the Papacy was in the hands of a series of French popes – the so-called 'Babylonian captivity'. Of all these popes, Clement was the most partisan, doling out senior Church positions to his relatives, friends and countrymen. Following on the heels of the rigid and austere Benedict XII, Clement sought to make the Church 'more accessible' and he did so with some style.

Born Pierre Roger, the former Benedictine monk had allegedly distinguished himself with his piety, but he was to abandon this as soon as he reached Peter's Chair. His pontificate was modelled less on the life of the Apostle and more on that of a carnal, temporal prince. He loved luxury and his reign was punctuated by sumptuous banquets and spectacular festivals. His frugal predecessor Benedict had built up the Vatican coffers and Clement now shamelessly depleted them.

He kept a harem of French whores about his chambers, and there were persistent rumours that he also liked the company of young boys. Rumoured to have been caught several times with married women, he is believed to have been treated several times for syphilis, insisting each time that physicians be blindfolded before they examined him. A consummate winebibber, he was unable to say Mass on a number of occasions due to drunkenness.

As the Black Death swept into Avignon, Clement died after a short illness but not before he had defended the Jews of the city who were accused of poisoning Christian wells – the last, charitable act of an otherwise sensual and licentious playboy Pope.

# THE JEWISH POPE

## Anacletus II
### FEBRUARY 1130–JANUARY 1138

'Is the Pope a Catholic?' runs the old answer in reply to some glaringly obvious question. Well, not always. In some instances, he may not even have been Christian. The first Pope, St Peter, was of course born and raised as a Jew but he was not the only pope of Jewish heritage.

Although not now recognised as a pope (but rather as an anti-pope), Pietro Pierloni was descended from a prominent family, which had converted to Christianity. Elected by the majority of his fellow cardinals, he was a controversial choice, because of his alleged connections with Judaism and allegations that he had bribed his way into the Papacy intending to destroy the Christian faith from the inside.

Those cardinals who had not voted for Anacletus elected another pope – Gregorio Papareschi, who took the name Innocent II. Both men were consecrated as pope on the same day. This started a schism in the Church, which was to last for eight years. Anacletus was backed by the powerful Roger II of Sicily whom he had quickly crowned, but Innocent enjoyed the support of Lothair III, the Holy Roman Emperor, Louis VI (Louis the Fat) of France and Henry I of England. Innocent, of course, had promised Lothair an imperial crown in return for his support.

21

The result was an unedifying spectacle as one pope excommunicated the other and racial insults such as 'Jew pope' and allegations of consorting with the Jews were tossed about. The strife and persecutions which ensued didn't die out even with Anacletus's death, and included threats of outright warfare.

In the face of such threats and the possibility of an attack on Rome by Lothair, his elected successor, Victor IV, surrendered to Innocent and resigned his position. Anacletus's name was subsequently struck from formal Vatican records as a 'Jewish traitor to Christendom'.

# THE EXHUMED POPE

## Formosus
### 6 OCTOBER 891–4 APRIL 896

It was not the politically controversial reign of Pope Formosus which made him notorious but rather the macabre events which occurred after his death. Having died at the age of eighty, Formosus was interred with all due ceremony in St Peter's. In January 897, however, one of his political enemies, who had become Pope Stephen VI, ordered his body to be exhumed and placed on trial for crimes against the Holy See.

By this time Formosus had been dead for nine months. Nonetheless, Stephen's order was carried out. The corpse was dug up, dressed in full pontificals and placed on a throne in front of a specially convened synod of cardinals.

Stephen charged it with a number of offences: that Formosus had become pope illegally, that he had abused his position as pontiff, that he had practised witchcraft and that he had taken bribes.

Stephen himself presided at the 'trial' and a deacon was appointed to answer the charges (in some accounts it is stated that he answered in an assumed voice) and to defend Formosus. Obviously, the defence was insufficient and the rotting corpse was found guilty, ritually stripped of its robes, had two fingers (with which the papal blessing was usually given) broken and other pieces of its anatomy mutilated. The corpse was then thrown into the River Tiber.

The whole absurd and grisly episode is often referred to as the 'Cadaver Synod' or the 'Synod Horrenda' and it did the Papacy no credit. Formosus's body was subsequently recovered from the Tiber by a hermit who reburied it in an unmarked grave.

Then, in 897, Theodore II reinstated Formosus and the body was exhumed once more! It was reburied in St Peter's.

# THE DEAD POPE

## Stephen II
**22 MARCH–24 MARCH 752**

At least Pope Formosus (*see above*) had the decency to die after his reign on the papal throne. The situation with Stephen II was somewhat different.

As the Papacy tried to split with the Byzantine Empire following the death of the Greek Pope Zachary, certain political factions hurriedly placed an elderly and ailing Roman priest on St Peter's Chair. The strain of the office was probably too much for the old man and it is thought that he died sometime during the service. Nevertheless, he was still invested as Pope, taking the name Stephen II, and celebrations commenced.

A day later it was announced that the Holy Father had suddenly died from a stroke and elections began again. It is thought that during all of Stephen's exceptionally brief reign (which is officially recorded as three days though it may well have been shorter), the Pope was actually dead.

Debate began to arise as to whether Stephen had been consecrated or been able to take his vows. Some Vatican officials assured the city that the Pope had been alive, but others questioned this. The Vatican was split on the subject.

This led to terrible confusion as to the order of popes who took the name Stephen. The dead pope's successor immediately took that name and also styled himself Stephen II, although until 1960 he was included in the *Annuario Pontificio* (the official list of popes) as Stephen III, the Vatican not wishing to acknowledge that the original Pope Stephen had been dead. This confusion continues down to the present day.

# THE ROBBER POPE

## Sergius II
**JANUARY 844–27 JANUARY 847**

Few pontificates have been as openly corrupt as that of Sergius II. Elderly, irascible and gouty, he assumed St Peter's Chair in late January 844. He was not a popular choice – the Roman people had already enthroned a likeable deacon named John as their next pontiff. However, through intimidation, bribery and false promises, Sergius secured the backing of the cardinals and the aristocracy and ousted the people's choice.

Rome threatened rebellion and Sergius was hurriedly elected without the formal acknowledgement of the Frankish court which was required by the Roman Constitution of 824 – a snub to the powerful Frankish emperor Lothair. In retaliation Lothair and his Frankish armies plundered papal territories and threatened Rome itself.

The emperor's son Louis brokered a deal which saved the city, but he found Sergius almost impossible to deal with – the Pope wanted a share of any tribute given by the Roman people to the Franks. Sergius's consecration went ahead and he anointed Louis as King of the Lombards.

The Pope and his brother Benedict now began careers of extortion and robbery. Although he wasn't the first pope to be in league with Roman criminals, Sergius's involvement with them ran very deep. He also shamelessly and publicly sold off bishoprics and other Church offices.

He was, it is believed, personally connected to a number of murders, and is thought to have taken out 'contracts' (paid assassinations) on many of his opponents. He weakened the Papacy so much that in August 846 Saracens successfully attacked and plundered St Peter and St Paul's cathedral – viewed by many contemporaries as Divine anger at papal corruption. Six months later in 847, Sergius died and was buried in St Peter's. There were few who mourned his passing.

# THE MURDEROUS POPE

## Sergius III
### 29 JANUARY 904–14 APRIL 911

Although Sergius II (*see above*) is thought to have been closely associated with criminals and assassins, he was nowhere near as vicious as one of his successors, the murderous Sergius III.

There is little doubt that he poisoned his predecessor who had been imprisoned by the anti-pope Christopher. Sergius also overthrew Christopher, had him imprisoned and poisoned him as well. Once in a position of power, Sergius brooked no opposition.

He reinstated the findings of the notorious *Cadaver Synod* (*see* The Exhumed Pope), overturning the appointments of Pope Formosus and throwing the entire Church into confusion. He further declared the date of his own 'election' as being 897 and denounced the ordinations of all popes since the time of Stephen VI (or VII, as the numbering of popes called Stephen has been unclear since Stephen II – *see* The Dead Pope) as invalid.

Those who spoke out against Sergius were either killed or thrown into prison. He remained close to one of the leading aristocratic Roman families who controlled several local militias and through this connection he kept his enemies in subjection. This, of course, did not stop him raping the fifteen-year-old daughter of the family and leaving her with child. This infant, a boy, would become the future Pope John XI, the only recorded illegitimate person to succeed to the Papacy.

So corrupt and licentious were Sergius and his successors that their collective reigns were referred to as 'the pornocracy'. Any sin could be forgiven by the Pope (who was not above sinning badly himself) as long as the offender had money to pay for that forgiveness.

He threw the Eastern Church into disarray by condoning the fourth marriage of the Byzantine Emperor Leo VI, in defiance of Eastern Canon Law. However, Leo was

prepared to pay the Pope a hefty sum for his support. The Patriarch of Constantinople, who had opposed the marriage, was deposed on the orders of the Pope and was forced into exile.

Sergius died in 911 after a brief illness and was succeeded by Anastasius III, who seems to have been less murderous but just as corrupt.

# THE PROMISCUOUS POPE

## John XII
### 16 DECEMBER 955–14 MAY 964

Although a number of popes were extremely promiscuous, one amongst them stands out. Elected at the age of eighteen, John XII's reign was dominated by his outrageous sexual behaviour.

He was elevated to the Papacy because of threats and promises made to the clergy by his dying father Alberic II, the effective ruler of all of Rome, and he was to die in his twenty-eighth year after a ten-year reign of sexual excess. It was said that there was no perversion which the Pope might not try and that he had consorted with young boys and animals within the Vatican precincts.

He was accused of turning the Lateran Palace into a brothel, so great were the numbers of prostitutes and paramours living there. It was whispered that the Holy Father allowed harlots to ply their trade within the Vatican itself as long as he received a percentage of their earnings.

John's behaviour became such a scandal that he was briefly removed from the Chair of St Peter by the unanimous vote of a synod. They elected a new Pope, Leo VIII, and John was forced to flee to Trivoli. However, Leo's rather dubious decrees proved unpopular with the Roman people. Within two months John was back in Rome, deposing Leo and taking the papal throne once more.

His sexual excesses continued unabated. Rumours that elderly and married women and small boys were entering the Pope's chambers circulated widely. With the reputation of the Vatican itself in danger, a synod of bishops called on the Pope to mend his personal ways. John didn't heed them.

One story states that during a papal procession through the streets of Rome, the extremely drunken Pope saw a young boy who took his eye and breaking from the procession pursued him through the crowd, hoisting up his robes as he

ran. Whether this is true or not (and there are indications that it might be), it gives an indication as to how the Papacy was viewed.

As the cardinals met to consider the future of the Papacy, John did the decent thing – he died. He had spent the day carousing with prostitutes and is reputed to have finished it in the bed of a married woman. The strain proved too much for him and he collapsed from a fatal heart attack, his body completely exhausted.

The cardinals immediately offered the Papacy to Leo VIII once again but by now the Holy Office was so mired in sleaze, controversy and outright filth that he refused it (he would not have been accepted by the Roman people anyway). Instead, one of the cardinal-deacons was elected to popular acclaim, as Benedict V. He was to reign for exactly one month.

# THE INCOMPETENT POPE

## Gregory XIV
### 5 DECEMBER 1590–16 OCTOBER 1591

The pontificate of Gregory XIV stands out in Papal history as one of the most unpopular and least successful. Although elected at the comparatively sprightly age of fifty-five, Gregory was often not in good health and was troubled with pains. He was something of a hypochondriac and had an almost paranoid distrust of those around him.

Because of his weak state and personal insecurities, the Curia allowed him to appoint his twenty-nine-year-old nephew, Paolo Emilio Sfondrati, as his Cardinal Secretary of State. Paolo, however, was completely corrupt, more interested in lining his own pockets than in running the Holy See in a proper fashion.

This was a time when Rome needed a strong pope – food shortages caused by foreign wars had left public morale very low and the Roman people looked to the Church for salvation and solace. What they got instead was exploitation. There seems little doubt that the Vatican was engaged in racketeering and may well have been operating a 'black market'.

Protestantism was on the march and the Pope's response to this was draconian. In an attempt to reassert Catholicism as the main religion of western Europe, he badly mishandled the situation – concentrating on minor infringements rather than establishing a logical and tolerant orthodoxy. He called for strict requirements for candidates to the hierarchy; he forbade Mass to be held in private houses; and he forbade the popular Roman sport of gambling on papal elections, the length of the pontificate and the number of cardinals created during a pope's reign.

These measures only served to alienate the public against the Papacy. Gregory further openly criticised the Protestant French King Henry IV, and his venom encouraged many moderate French Catholics to take Henry's side.

Gregory stoked up the rivalry between France and Spain, firmly allying himself with Catholic Spain and threatening to precipitate a war in Western Europe.

In the face of both public and political displeasure, Gregory took to his bed, claiming ill-health, and left the running of the Papacy largely to his corrupt nephew. As the crisis deepened, Paolo's handling grew more inept and Gregory increasingly withdrew from the affairs of the Vatican, except to deliver extreme pronouncements, which hindered more than they helped.

In the end, he simply gave up and died as the winter of 1591 approached, leaving the mess that he'd created to his successor, Innocent IX, who was to reign for just two months.

# THE UNSTABLE POPE

## Urban VI
### 8 APRIL 1378–15 OCTOBER 1389

Although madness has never been a disqualification for the Papacy and indeed a number of popes, such as Stephen VI(I), were clearly deranged, the pontificate of Urban VI displayed a much more subtle mental instability.

Subject to violent mood swings and with an almost maniacal temper, by the summer of 1378 Urban had alienated most of the cardinals who had elected him. In fact, he was so unreasonable that few cardinals would even approach him.

Born Bartolomeo Prignano, prior to his election Urban had been a competent and efficient administrator. However, as soon as he became pontiff he began to display an alarming side to his nature. He began to shout and roar filthy abuse at those who disagreed with him on the slightest matter. Sometimes, he would physically attack them.

Faced with such uncontrollable tirades, on 1 August 1378 the French cardinals published a declaration that the Pope's election had been invalid, and they invited Urban to abdicate. The Pope, of course, refused, denouncing the cardinals in a stream of written obscenities.

On 30 October the cardinals elected Robert of Geneva, the French King's cousin, as Pope Clement VII. Urban denounced him as a heretic and excommunicated him; Clement replied in similar fashion and Europe's loyalties were now badly divided between them. This opened up what was to become known as the Great Western Schism, which was to continue until the Council of Constance (1414–18), by which time there was a *third* Pope, Martin V.

In a fit of anger, Urban ordered his forces (the armies of those who were loyal to him) to attack the lands of Clement's supporters. When the response was not what he had hoped for, he hired armed mercenaries. Urban's forces achieved a victory near Marino in April 1379, captured the Castel San Angelo and occupied most of the city of Rome.

Horrified by the Pope's actions and his increasingly violent temper, the majority of the Holy Curia defected to Clement. Urban excommunicated them all and organised a new Curia but he soon fell out with that as well.

As the crisis deepened, Urban chose to ignore it and set about securing the Kingdom of Naples for one of his nephews. In 1380, he excommunicated and deposed Queen Joanna for having supported Clement. He then personally crowned her cousin, Charles of Durazzo.

However, he soon took a dislike to Charles, who began to plot with the exiled cardinals to overthrow Urban on the grounds of mental instability. On hearing of the conspiracy, Urban preached a crusade against Naples and placed the entire Kingdom under interdict, depriving it of spiritual and sacramental benefits.

He was now obsessed with removing Charles from the monarchy and, declaring himself a Soldier of Christ, personally led an assault on the King's stronghold at Nocera. Urban was no military commander and Charles escaped, but the Pope's mercenary forces took five cardinals prisoner. Urban threw them into prison, where he had them tortured and finally executed.

The Vatican coffers now being completely depleted, he was forced to return to Rome where by various bizarre decrees he rapidly alienated the people.

With the Papal States in a condition of confusion and anarchy and the Papacy itself tainted with a vindictive madness, Urban VI suddenly died. It is quite probable that he was poisoned. At the time of his death, Clement VII was still alive in Avignon but there was no real interest in recognising him as the legitimate pope. The Western Schism continued.

# DEBAUCHED POPES

## Innocent VIII
### 29 AUGUST 1484–29 JULY 1492

With the pontificate of Innocent VIII, the Papacy plumbed new depths of debauchery, laying the foundation for the even more hedonistic Papacy that followed. There was nothing holy or even vaguely sanctified about Innocent's reign, nor anything to distinguish the Vatican from the court of a sensual, worldly prince.

Because of immense debts left by his predecessor Sixtus IV, Innocent had to use unscrupulous methods to raise money to maintain his own lavish lifestyle and that of his cardinals. He created new and unnecessary offices in the Curia which he then sold off for exorbitant prices. He held auctions for existing offices which were sold to the highest bidder. This was, of course, the sin of simony against which previous popes had spoken out.

Foolishly, he threatened the powerful Ferdinand I of Naples, who had refused to pay the recently raised papal taxes. Innocent allied himself with barons who were fomenting rebellion against the Neapolitan King. When the threatened rebellion crumbled, the Pope was forced to make a humiliating and personally distasteful peace with Ferdinand in 1486.

Like a number of other popes, Innocent had several mistresses and it is known that some of these bore him children whom he openly acknowledged. In fact, his son Franceschetto was married to the daughter of Lorenzo de Medici, a member of one of the leading Roman houses. The Pope made their thirteen-year-old son – his grandson – a cardinal at the age of thirteen.

As early opposition to his hedonistic reign grew, Innocent decided to divert it by appearing to take religious action. He therefore targeted alleged witches in Germany, issuing the famous Papal Bull *Summis desiderantes* on 5 December 1484. He also strengthened the arm of the Holy Inquisition and commissioned Heinrich Kramer (former senior Inquisitor in the Tyrol) and the theologian Jacobus Sprenger to write the Church's foremost manual against witchcraft, *Malleus Malificarum* (The Hammer of the Witch), which has remained a classic ever since.

He began to preach a crusade against the Turks. But in contravention of his own call, he made a peace with the Turkish Sultan, accepting the Sultan's half-brother as hostage as well as a personal payment of about one million pounds (forty thousand ducats) per year. He also received the Spear of Longinus, which was supposed to have pierced the side of Christ on the Cross.

Innocent received some respite from the criticism that attended his reign with the news that the Moorish caliphate of Granada had fallen to Christian forces. He therefore proclaimed the Spanish King Ferdinand and his Queen Isabella and their descendants as 'Catholic kings'. He then returned to his drinking and whoring.

His hedonistic lifestyle was taking its toll, however – the Pope was now frequently drunk and was becoming increasingly unable to fulfil his duties. Three days before Christopher Columbus reached the coast of America, Innocent fell ill. It is said that as he lay dying on 25 July 1492, he told the cardinals around his bed that his reign had been one of debauchery and sin and begged them to elect a pope who was better than he. It's a pity that they didn't heed him.

## Alexander VI
### 26 AUGUST 1492–18 AUGUST 1503

If Innocent was bad, his successor was to become the most notorious pope in history. The second of two Spanish popes, he was born Rodrigo de Borja y Borja (or Borgia in its Italian translation) and was the nephew of Pope Callistus III, who had made him a cardinal-deacon at the age of twenty-five.

Ambitious and greedy, he had lived a corrupt and promiscuous life before becoming Pope. In order to become pontiff, he offered generous bribes, together with promises of lucrative appointments and benefices. His election was therefore simonical (purchased) and could have been declared invalid, but nobody opposed him. Taking the name Alexander VI, he was crowned in St Peter's in 1492.

He made a promising start, inevitably calling for a crusade against the Turks and promising to reform a thoroughly corrupt Curia. However, it soon became evident that the Pope was more concerned with impregnating female consorts and doling out positions and privileges to his relatives than with sacred matters.

For example, he made one son, Cesare, a cardinal at the age of eighteen, even though he was linked with gambling and extortion throughout Rome. He further made a cardinal of the brother of one of the whores who visited his bedchamber.

He often left the Papacy in the hands of his daughter, Lucrezia, whilst he was away from Rome with his concubines. He arranged several advantageous marriages for Lucrezia with wealthy husbands who died shortly after – Lucrezia Borgia is known to history as a famous poisoner.

Alexander is perhaps best remembered for a political act in 1493, when he drew the line of demarcation between the Spanish and Portuguese zones of exploration in the New World, which had to be revised the following year as the Pope had, not surprisingly, erred substantially in favour of the Spanish.

His personal life, meanwhile, became more and more scandalous – prostitutes came and went from the Vatican with an almost monotonous regularity. The celebrated Florentine preacher and reformer Girolamo Savonarola called for the overthrow of Alexander and a return to moral ways, and the Pope's response to this was to have

Savonarola excommunicated. He was arrested, horribly tortured and finally executed.

Others were now frightened to speak out against him, even as Alexander squandered Vatican money on the lavish decoration of his own apartments and those of his family.

Following the death of his favourite son Juan in June 1497 (probably poisoned by his own brother Cesare), Alexander was so devastated that he publicly vowed to live a more upright life and to concern himself with Church reform. However, unable to resist the temptations of the flesh, he soon forgot his vow and filled the Vatican with whores. He also 'lent' Vatican money to his family, enabling them to buy estates for themselves. The Borgias were now treating the Holy See like a personal bank.

One evening Alexander and Cesare attended a supper given for them by a cardinal. Both of them accidentally ingested a large amount of poison, which was reputedly meant for their host – some say that Alexander himself had planted it in the food but had mistakenly eaten the wrong portion. The Pope died but his son survived. Vatican records piously state that the Holy Father died of a fever which was raging in Rome at the time, but this is almost certainly not the case.

He was buried in the Chapel of San Andrea in St Peter's, but around 1610 his remains were exhumed and transferred to the Spanish church of Santa Maria di Monserrato in Rome. He left a Church badly divided and mired in controversy and was succeeded by a sickly, compromise, stopgap pope, Pius III.

# THE EGOTISTICAL POPE

## Boniface VIII
### 25 JANUARY 1295–11 OCTOBER 1303

Benedetto Caetani, or Boniface VIII, was known by his contemporaries as a scheming, vicious and thoroughly nasty pope. He had tricked his predecessor, Celestine V, out of the Papacy through a mixture of bribes, promises and threats.

He may have called himself Boniface but his opponents declared that he certainly did not have a 'bonny face'. Pinched and perpetually scowling, the new pope was hardly an approachable figure.

Boniface had grandiose ideas about his holy office and of his own competence within it. He dressed in full pontifical robes on every occasion, no matter how small, and declared himself as powerful as any king or emperor. He treated everyone who came near him with a disdainful attitude, which outraged many of the powerful noble Roman families.

Above all, Boniface saw himself as an important figure on the world's stage. He tried to meddle, mostly ineffectively, in the political affairs of other countries, offering, for instance, to defend Scotland's independence from England and to restore Charles II of Naples to the throne of Sicily. All of these schemes came to nothing.

The main confrontation in Boniface's pontificate, however, was with Philip IV (Philip the Fair), a man who was as self-opinionated as the Pope himself. Boniface had no love for the French king and thought to 'cut him down to size' by forbidding the taxation of clergy upon which Philip relied to finance his foreign wars. An imperious Papal Bull, *Clericis Laicos*, was issued on 25 February 1296, aimed at the French King.

It was a stupid move, for the Vatican revenues partly depended on the export of gold from France – exports which Philip promptly withheld. Boniface was humiliatingly forced to back down and in 1297 allowed the French King to tax the clergy once more without consulting the Holy See.

Boniface became ever more grandiose, eventually declaring himself more powerful than any temporal ruler. In 1301, this re-ignited the feud with Philip IV, who immediately imprisoned the Bishop of Parmiers and demanded his reduction to a lay status. Considering this an imposition on his spiritual authority, Boniface convened a synod to denounce the King. Thirty-nine French bishops attended despite Philip's order not to. From this synod emerged the Papal Bull *Unam Sanctum*, by which Boniface reasserted his authority and concentrated yet more power in his own hands.

Philip responded with a tirade of abuse directed against the Pope. His charges, all of which were probably true, included simony, sexual misconduct, blasphemy, usurping of papal office and heresy. Philip called for a grand council to impeach the Pope and depose him.

Despite his haughtiness, Boniface had no wish to face such a gathering and after preparing a Bull of Excommunication against the king, he fled from Rome to the papal palace at Anagni, the city of his birth. He was, however, pursued by armed mercenaries. The palace was stormed and, refusing to resign, Boniface was taken prisoner, dressed in his full pontifical robes.

Even in captivity he treated his captors with cold disdain – he was the Pope after all! They had planned to take him to France to be tried as a common criminal but the citizens of Anagni managed to rescue him after three days. After a period of rest, Boniface returned to Rome, but his spirit was crushed and he died less than three weeks later, on 12 October 1303.

Boniface is believed by some historians to have invented the Pope's Ring – a device with a poisoned spike on its lower side which pricked the skin of enemies as they kissed it – though that invention has been attributed to a number of other popes, including Alexander VI.

Boniface exhausted the Papacy in useless political strife to serve his own ego and although other pontiffs were more corrupt, few can have moved it further from the original humble ideals of St. Peter.

# THE BEWILDERED POPE

## St Celestine V
### 29 AUGUST–13 DECEMBER 1294

Although he could hardly be considered a worldly, cruel or evil pope, Celestine V was clearly out of his depth in the Papacy. His ordination came about in a particularly curious way.

Following the death of Nicholas IV, the Curia was badly split over a possible successor. Negotiations dragged on for weeks and months and, with no one sitting in St Peter's Chair, the very tradition of the Papacy itself was in danger.

Seeing an opportunity for himself, the Cardinal-priest of San Martino, Benedetto Caetani, suddenly turned up with a letter written in a curious and unintelligible script. The Cardinal claimed that this was a letter from God, instructing the Curia to elect him (Caetani) as pope. The Curia were understandably suspicious and took the letter to a venerable old Benedictine hermit, Pietro del Murrone, who was living in a cave outside the city. The hermit studied the document and declared that it was indeed from God, but it said that he (Pietro) should be pope.

The hermit was immediately declared the next Pontiff, taking the name Celestine V, and was brought back to Rome in triumph. He entered the city seated upon a donkey, in imitation of Christ. He was accompanied by Charles II, King of Sicily and Naples, who had lost no time ingratiating himself with the new Pope.

Benedetto Caetani was furious. Even though Celestine was now eighty years old and his pontificate was not expected to be a long one, Caetani resolved to make his life miserable. However, he needn't have worried. The new Pope was still a simple monk at heart and was overwhelmed by the magnificence and pomp of his surroundings.

The papal office was not only a spiritual calling, it was a political one as well and Celestine had to deal with the complicated Roman political landscape and its feuding clans of wealthy families. He naively became a pawn of Charles II who saw to it that Celestine took up residency in Naples at Castel Nuovo.

To the alarm of the Curia, the Pope began to give away part of the Vatican wealth to beggars in the Neapolitan streets. It was a laudable and exemplary act of Christian charity but it alarmed the Vatican financiers.

After years of living alone in a cave, Celestine's personal habits left a lot to be desired. He slobbered when he ate; he never washed and he 'eased himself' as he sat on the papal throne, sitting for long periods in his own ordure, lost in holy contemplation. He literally stank and, with princes and dignitaries visiting, this was not an image that the Vatican wished to present.

Taking advantage of the Pope's bewilderment at his new office, Benedetto Caetani, who was a skilled papal lawyer, suggested to Celestine that he should resign. Of course, should this happen Caetani planned to run as pope himself. Celestine, however, replied that as God had instructed him to be Pope, only God could instruct him to resign the office.

So Caetani tried another trick. Taking a room directly over the papal apartments, he drilled a small hole in the floor. Each night as Celestine retired, Caetani would put his mouth to the hole and whisper, 'Celestine! Celestine! This is the voice of the Holy Spirit. The office that you have accepted is too great for you to bear! Give up the Papacy and return to your hermitage! This is the express will of God. And you must also publicly name Benedetto Caetani as your successor. God wishes him to be the next pope.'

For several nights, Caetani repeated these instructions until, at last, the bewildered Pope decided to abdicate. Celestine accepted the formula for abdication that Caetani had prepared for him and vacated the papal throne, leaving the way open for the unscrupulous lawyer.

Shortly afterwards Caetani became Pope, taking the name Boniface VIII. He did not, however, allow his predecessor to return to his hermitage but, fearing that he would prove a rallying point for malcontents, had him placed under guard and thrown into Castel Fumone, east of Ferentino, where the old monk eventually died of an abscess that had turned septic.

Celestine was buried in Ferentino but his remains were transferred in 1517 to Santa Maria di Collemaggio in L'Aquila, where he had been crowned Pope. He was later canonised by Pope Clement V, under the direct orders of the French King Philip IV, who had been a dedicated opponent of Boniface VIII.

# THE FEMALE POPE?

## John VIII?
### 855–7 APRIL 858?

Throughout medieval history and beyond, the legend of a female pope or 'Pope Joan' persisted and was equated with the pontificate of John VIII. The dates for 'Pope Joan', however, do not correspond with the official Vatican records for the reign of John VIII (14 December 872–16 December 882).

Her alleged dates, however, roughly correspond with the reign of Benedict III, a pope about whose reign very little seems to be known. Some authorities state that the legend of the female pope springs from some of the debaucheries carried out by John XII (see The Promiscuous Pope), who reputedly enjoyed dressing as a woman from time to time.

According to some traditions, there were *two* John VIIIs, one of whom ruled briefly during the pontificate attributed to Benedict III and whose name was struck from papal records. This is usually offered as a reason why there is no John XX – the number was omitted in order to bring Vatican records into line.

According to the legend, an Englishwoman (other versions of the story say that she was born in Mainz in Germany) made her way to Rome, via Athens, disguised as a monk and called herself (or studied under someone called) John

Angelicus. She had a brilliant career in Vatican circles and was unanimously elevated to the Papacy, taking the name John VIII.

She allegedly reigned for two years and seven months (although other versions give a shorter period). However, it is alleged that she was sexually promiscuous and during an Easter procession near the Basilica of San Clemente she was suddenly taken ill, falling to the pavement. The reason for her discomfort soon became clear as she gave birth in front of the astonished cardinals, thus revealing her true gender. Directly following the birth, she was literally torn limb from

limb by an outraged Roman mob (other versions say that she was imprisoned and was later stoned to death).

Yet more variations on the theme say that her reign directly followed that of Victor III in 1087, but no record of it exists. All reference to it was struck off by her successor, allegedly Benedict III, in an act of *damnato memoriae*.

The tale of 'Pope Joan' seems to have first appeared in a work by Stephen of Bourbon (*d*.1261) entitled *De Septum Donis Spiritus Sancti* (The Seven Gifts of the Holy Spirit), and was then taken up by a number of other medieval writers.

The alleged reign has led to another intriguing piece of papal folklore. Following the accession of a female pontiff, it was said that all newly-elected popes had to submit to an inspection to ensure their masculinity.

They were required to sit on a chair with a hole in its centre while a specially appointed cardinal felt underneath to satisfy himself that the pontiff was masculine. This was done in full view of the electing cardinals and when the cry was heard, '*Testicules habit*' ('He has testicles'), everyone joyfully proceeded to the consecration. This, it is said, is no longer Vatican procedure and the last pope to submit himself to this indignity is believed to have been Pius XII.

Photographs purporting to be of the special chair used in this procedure have been published in a number of books and magazines. Whether or not these are genuine and whether the chair was used for the purpose described is unclear.

There may well have been some procedure for examining the gender of newly elected popes but it is likely to have pre-dated the time of 'Pope Joan'. Indeed, it was probably the fear of some female usurping the Holy Office that gave rise to the legend of a female pope in the first place.

# THE PASTA-LOVING POPE

## John XXIII
### OCTOBER 1958–3 JUNE 1963

In their daily lives, popes are expected to be austere and to show restraint towards worldly things. This usually means that they eat in moderation, eschewing the worldly pleasures of the laden table.

Certainly this could not be said about Angelo Roncalli, who was to become Pope John XXIII, one of the most beloved pontiffs in history. He was extremely fond of his food and, as an Italian, he had a particular love of pasta. He couldn't get enough of it!

Late at night – John famously needed very little sleep – he would prowl the Vatican kitchens, raiding the fridges as he went. In the early hours of the morning, he was sometimes found, in full pontifical robes, devouring huge platefuls of spaghetti and tomato sauce.

John was an extremely popular pope and one devoted to healing the divisions between the Catholic and Protestant churches. When he died, the Union Jack flew at half-mast even in the pro-Unionist, anti-Catholic city of Belfast.

However, his ecumenist stance made him unpopular amongst conservatives within the Vatican, so when it was suggested that he be made a saint, the issue was derided by his detractors, because 'the Holy Father had given in to the awful sin of gluttony'. His late-night pasta had come back to haunt him!

He was not, however, as big a glutton as Pius V (?–1572), who absolutely adored food and was apparently an excellent cook. Indeed, his most widely sought-after work was not a papal encyclical but a cookbook, *The Cooking Secrets of Pope Pius V,* which was something of a bestseller of its day.

# THE PENNY-PINCHING POPE

## Pius XII
### 2 MARCH 1939–9 OCTOBER 1958

Across the years, many popes have been noted for their great extravagance. Few pontiffs have actually been celebrated for their frugality. But when it came to miserliness, very few people could match Pope Pius XII.

Born Eugenio Maria Giovanni Pacelli, he was the son of a lawyer who seems to have taught him the 'virtue' of penny-pinching, a characteristic that he brought to the Papacy. 'I can never,' he is said to have declared, 'be extravagant with the funds of the Holy See. God would never forgive me.'

To this end, he would wander through the Vatican at night, turning off all lights that had been inadvertently left on. All telephone calls within the Vatican, even on the smallest business, had to be logged and accounted for and he issued a decree that all envelopes used in Vatican communications had to be sealed in such a way that they could be reused. He also refused to make certain essential repairs to the Vatican itself for fear of spending money – he automatically assumed that all builders were rogues.

On his death it was found that he had even written his own papal will on the back of an envelope which had previously been used for something else. Although he was personally very frugal – 'penny wise' – his administration squandered money on various initiatives which came to nothing and which were ill-thought out – 'pound foolish'.

# THE POOL-PLAYING POPE

## Pius IX
### JUNE 1848–7 FEBRUARY 1878

If the idea of the pontiff as a pool-hall hustler appals you, then it is probably better that you ignore some of the aspects of the papal reign of Pius IX.

Giovanni Maria Mastai-Ferrettu, who began his career as a soldier in the Vatican Guard even though his father was a count who could have ensured him religious office, was the longest-serving pope in history. He also convened the First Vatican Council, which confirmed the doctrine of Papal Infallibility.

BLACK BALL, TOP RIGHT HAND POCKET.

DEAR SWEET HOLY MARY, JESUS AND ALL THE SAINTS PLEASE LET HIM MISS IT...

Whilst a soldier, he developed an interest in both billiards and pool, which turned into something of an obsession. Upon becoming Pope, he promptly installed two billiard tables – one in his retreat at Castel Gandolfo and one in the Vatican itself. He was a skilled and cunning player, insisting that many of his cardinals learn how to play the game so that he could play against them – he invariably beat them. He also played regularly against members of the Vatican Guard.

It is also known, though not publicly admitted, that he played for money, which would certainly be a sin in papal terms! It has been remarked that, both in style and temperament, Pius IX would not have looked out of place in the pool halls of the Lower Bronx in New York – now there's an image to conjure with!

# THE HYPOCHONDRIAC POPE

## Pius XII
**MARCH 1939–9 OCTOBER 1958**

Besides being known as something of a skinflint, Pius XII was widely regarded as a hypochondriac. He imagined himself to be suffering from a variety of ailments, and was particularly fearful of dental infections.

Consequently, the simple act of cleaning his teeth became a long and complicated ritual. First, he used a special toothpaste, prepared for him by a chemist in Rome. He then cleaned his mouth using a strong astringent, finally massaging his gums with sterilised cotton dipped in a mild disinfectant.

Convinced that his gums were still bad and refusing to take the advice of the Vatican doctors, Pius sought out a Roman dentist, by all accounts little more than a quack, who prescribed a 'remedy' for him using chromic acid – an extremely powerful substance, which was commonly used to tan hides.

Frequent applications of this caused the Pope's gums to become more and more sensitive and also acted upon the Pontiff like a subtle poison, causing stomach disorders and spasms, which Pius ascribed to his own failing body. He also suffered from severe attacks of hiccups.

Pius had a morbid fear of flies and insects and often kept a fly swatter about his person. However, before swatting a fly, the swatter had to be dipped in disinfectant lest some infection would be transmitted as it was being killed. By the time Pius had completed this ritual, the fly had usually gone. To insects, the Pope ascribed bilious attacks and imagined liver disorders.

He actually did suffer from chronic gastritis, brought on, according to Vatican doctors, by his nervous disposition. Throughout his pontificate, however, Pius claimed to have a mysterious 'chronic toothache', an irregular pulse, an imagined heart disorder and an ulcer.

He died quietly at Castel Gandolfo in October 1958, reputedly complaining of ill health up until the end. This time, however, he was right!

# THE SOCCER-MAD POPE

## John Paul II
**OCTOBER 1978–10 FEBRUARY 2005**

Although the ritual of the papal inauguration has been established over centuries, at his inauguration Pope John Paul II dispensed with tradition by bringing the holy ceremony forward by several hours and slightly shortening it. The reason for this was that the new Pope, who was an ardent soccer fan, wished to see an important football match on television.

# THE MISNUMBERED POPE?

## Benedict XVI
**APRIL 2005–**

When Joseph Ratzinger took the name Benedict XVI in April 2005, he may have made a mistake; he may only have been Benedict XV. However, a number of his predecessors, taking the same name, may have done likewise. The problem arises with Benedict X (d.1059).

By the eleventh century the Papacy was in political chaos. A series of pontiffs imposed by the German King Henry III had come to an end with Victor II. Taking advantage of Henry's death and the fact that his son Henry IV was only a child, the Roman families elected a pope of their own choice – Stephen IX – on 2 August 1057, without notifying the Imperial German Court.

His weak and faltering reign came to an end on 29 March 1058, but not before he had named a successor – an advisor named Hildebrand, who was then in Germany negotiating peace and reform with the German Court.

Fearing that Hildebrand might make too many concessions, an anti-reformist group of Roman families elected a pope in his absence – John, Cardinal-Bishop of Valletri – who took the name Benedict X. The new Pope took office on 5 April

1058. The Curia now descended into unseemly squabbling and feuding, with allegations of bribery and political feuding.

Word reached Hildebrand in Germany as he negotiated with the Regent there, the Empress Agnes. He could not return to claim the pontificate but nominated Gerard, Bishop of Florence, as the next pope. Gerard was duly elected in Siena in December 1058, taking the name Nicholas II and promptly excommunicating Benedict. Backed by armies from sympathetic nobles, Nicholas entered Rome and forced Benedict to flee.

However, Benedict still had some supporters – including Gerard of Galaria – and mounted his own army to retake Rome. Nicholas's army marched to meet with them and the armies clashed. The battle of Campagna in 1059 was not as conclusive as Nicholas would have hoped but Benedict conceded the Papacy and denounced himself as a heretic. He further declared that he had never been pope.

In return for this admission, Nicholas allowed him to go free but when Hildebrand returned from Germany in 1060, he had Benedict arrested as a traitor to the Church and imprisoned until he died, in either 1073 or 1080. Hildebrand, who would later become Pope Gregory VII, declared that there never had been a pope named Benedict X and that all reference to him should be excised from Vatican records.

This remained the situation until the pontificate of Niccolo Boccasini, Cardinal-Bishop of Ostia, in October 1303. He chose the name Benedict, which had been the baptismal name of his predecessor Boniface VIII. The Curia pleaded with him to take the papal name of Benedict X, but he refused and took the name of Benedict XI in defiance of Hildebrand's instructions. Technically this was heresy as it contravened Church doctrine and implied a recognition of Benedict X's claim to the Papacy, but no action was taken against him.

However, even today, Vatican records pass directly from Benedict IX to Benedict XI with no mention of Benedict X.

Benedict XII, a French pope elected in Avignon, reigned from 1335–42. There were then two popes named Benedict XIII, the first another Avignon pontiff who reigned from 1394–1407, during the Great Western Schism. The second Benedict XIII reigned from 1724–30. Pietro Francisco Orsini actually denounced the Avignon pope before assuming his name. He had originally considered taking the name Benedict XIV, but realised that this would have legitimised the French pontiff.

Benedict XIV reigned from 1740–58, and Benedict XV from 1914–22. So, by adopting the title Benedict XVI instead of Benedict XV, did Joseph Ratzinger, along with these other Benedicts, commit heresy by implicitly acknowledging the reign of Benedict X? An intriguing question and one perhaps only the Vatican itself can answer.

# THE SCHOLAR POPE

## John XXI
**SEPTEMBER 1276–20 MAY 1277**

The only Portuguese pope to date, Petrus Hispanus (Peter of Spain) was a renowned theological scholar. He was also academically vain, boasting a huge library of Scriptural works.

Immediately on becoming Pope, he had a small library built at the rear of the papal palace in Viterbo to house his large collection. In order to please the impatient Pope, the library was hastily constructed and almost as soon as John retired to

IRONIC REALLY, HE WAS ALWAYS BURIED IN HIS BOOKS WHEN HE WAS ALIVE AS WELL.

it in order to study, the ceiling caved in and the books piled against the walls fell on top of him.

He suffered fearful injuries from which he died two days later. It is therefore true to say that the Pope's scholarliness was the death of him.

STRUCK-OFF POPES: **JOHN XX**

**THE EX-CON POPE:** **CA**

THE SUED POPE: **PAUL VI** **CA**

**NONEXISTENT POPES**

MARRIED POPES: **HORMIS**

**PLAYBOY POPI**

**CLEMEN**

**ANACLETUS II** THE EXHUME

**THE DEAD PO**

**SERGIUS II** THE MURDER

THE PROMISCUOUS POPE: **JOHN XII** THE IN

**THE UNSTABLE POPE**

**ALEXANDER VI** THE EGOTISTICAL POPE:

ST CELESTINE V **THE FEMALE**

**JOHN XXIII** THE PI

THE HYPOCHONDRIAC POPE:

THE MISNUMBERED POPE?: **BENEDICT XVI** THE SO